Divers' Dream

TAIOMA

by **Angie Belcher**
photographs by **Andy Belcher**

Learning Media®

Contents

1. *The Two-dollar Tug*

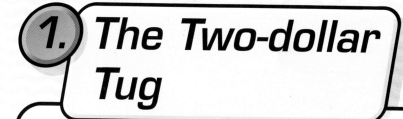

A tugboat is a very strong boat. It often pulls bigger boats along. "Tug" is another word for "pull." Tugboats are sometimes called "tugs" for short.

This tugboat is called the *Taioma*. (Say it "Tie-o-ma.")

In the past, it carried heavy loads and towed many boats.

It pulled many big ships in and out of **harbors**.

The *Taioma* became old and rusty.
No one wanted it anymore.

A businessman saw the *Taioma* in the harbor and had an idea. He bought the tug for only two dollars.

Another tug towed the *Taioma* for 540 miles to the bay where the businessman lived. He put the *Taioma* in the town's museum.

People visited the tug for many years. Then the museum closed. Once again, no one wanted the tug.

2. Saving the Tug

A **scuba diver** called Steve saw the tug.
It gave him an idea. He wanted to sink
the *Taioma* in the ocean for divers to visit.

A newspaper reporter wrote a story about what Steve wanted to do.

Plans for Tug

The tug *Taioma* has been in the museum for many years. But it may soon return to the ocean.

Scuba diver Steve Weidmann plans to sink the tug in the ocean.

"I want to turn the tug into a place for my friends and me to go diving. It will be a dream come true for us," said Steve.

Some people wrote letters to the **editor** at the newspaper.

Dear Editor

I think that making the *Taioma* into a place for diving is a great idea. It will make a good home for fish.

Ben Roberts

Dear Editor

The *Taioma* should NOT be sunk. Why does everyone want to dump their trash in the ocean?

Patsy Jones

DON'T
DUMP
TRASH

NO SWIMMING
OR DIVING
OF ANY KIND

3. *Problem Solving*

Steve thought about all the problems he might have.

Problem One: Will the *Taioma* harm **marine life**?

Solution: Steve asked some **marine biologists** to look at marine life in the area. This is what they said:

Marine life will not be harmed. In fact, a lot of marine life will probably want to live in the tug. Please clean the tug carefully before you sink it.

Problem Two: How will the tugboat be moved to the ocean?

Solution: Engineers will help Steve to work out a plan.

Problem Three: How will such a heavy boat be moved?

Solution: Make the tug lighter by taking everything off it. Cut out the portholes and cut off the top of the funnel.

funnel

portholes

Problem Four: How can a tug be moved along a busy road?

Solution: Move it at night when there are fewer cars. Ask the police to stop traffic and close the roads.

4. On the Move

Two trucks and a long flatbed trailer with 128 wheels arrived at the old museum.

The tug was sitting on concrete blocks. Workers put four huge **jacks** under the tug to lift it up off the blocks.

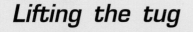

Lifting the tug

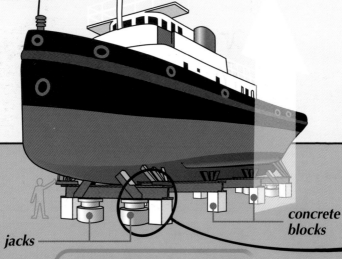

jacks

concrete blocks

Jacks are placed underneath the tug.

The workers lifted the back of the tug four inches off the ground. Then they lifted the front four inches off the ground. The workers did this over and over again. Then they put some wooden blocks between the tug and the concrete blocks.

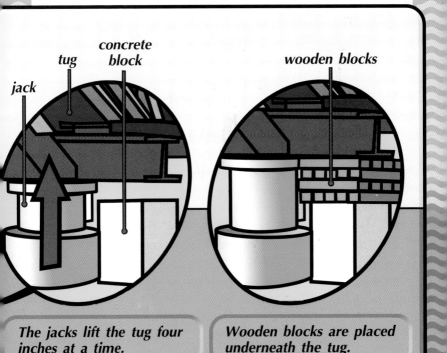

jack

tug

concrete block

wooden blocks

The jacks lift the tug four inches at a time.

Wooden blocks are placed underneath the tug.

When the tug was high enough, a driver backed the flatbed trailer underneath the tug. Then the jacks were lowered until the tug was sitting on the trailer.

This map shows the route from the museum to the harbor.

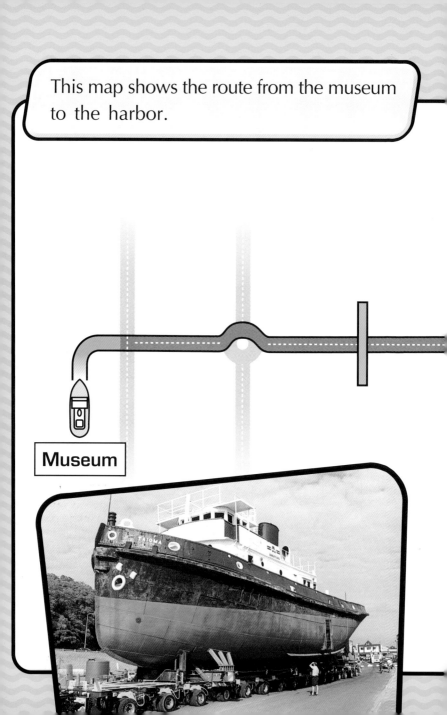

Museum

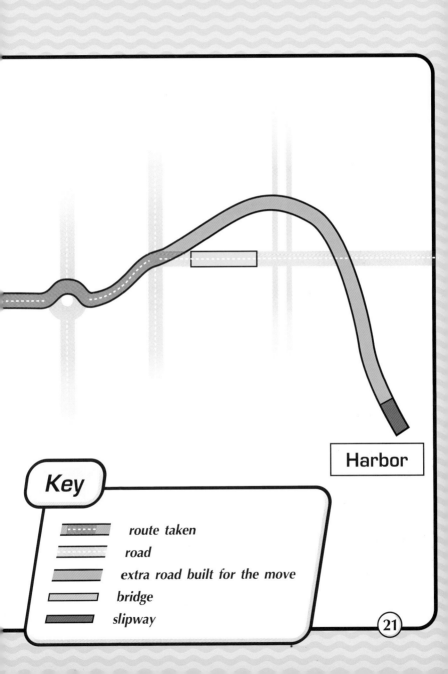

Harbor

Key

route taken
road
extra road built for the move
bridge
slipway

21

Kelsey Carter read about the *Taioma* in the newspaper. Kelsey's mom took her to watch the tugboat on the move.

Kelsey wrote about what she saw.

THE BIG MOVE

by Kelsey Carter

10:00 p.m. It was dark. The police stopped the traffic.

10:30 p.m. The *Taioma* began to move.

11:00 p.m. The tug reached a bridge that went over the road. The tug couldn't fit underneath it. So some workers unbolted the bridge. A big **crane** lifted the bridge so the tug could go through.

Midnight A streetlight blocked the way. Steve climbed onto the tug and cut off its rails. The sparks were like fireworks.

2:00 a.m. – 4:00 a.m. The tug kept moving toward the harbor.

5:00 a.m. The tug reached the harbor. The driver backed the trailer into the water. The tug floated into the ocean. Another tug helped push the *Taioma* up the **slipway**.

Steve and his friends cleaned the tug. They **welded** the doorways open so divers would be able to find their way around safely. Steve cut four holes in the side of the tug. The holes needed to be blocked while the *Taioma* was being towed out to the ocean. Later, they would be unblocked to let the water in.

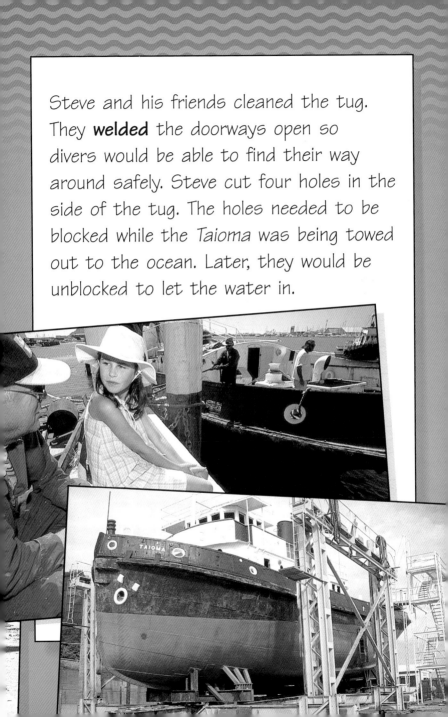

5. Out to the Ocean

Two tugs towed the *Taioma* out of the harbor. One tug pulled, and the other tug pushed.

Motiti Island

Taioma sunk here

When the *Taioma* was in the right place, the people on the two tugs untied the ropes. Steve unblocked the holes he had cut and climbed off the *Taioma*.

Water rushed in through the holes, and the *Taioma* began to sink.

When the tug had sunk, Steve and his friends dived down to take a look.

The old tugboat that nobody had wanted was now a divers' dream.

Glossary

(These words are printed in bold type the first time they appear in the book.)

crane: a machine that lifts heavy things

editor: a person in charge of making a newspaper

engineer: a person who plans how to make things like bridges and roads

harbor: a bay that boats come into

jack: a tool that is used to lift something

marine biologist: a person who studies creatures that live in the ocean

marine life: creatures that live in the ocean

scuba diver: a person who swims underwater using air in a tank to breathe

slipway: a place where ships are fixed

weld: to join metal together using heat

Index